Those Roaring Riverboat Years

A History of the Steamboat Era

As told by the greatest river pilots who ever lived
Capt. Edward Heckmann
[his actual voice, who had license to pilot more river that anyone before or since]
and **MarkTwain**,
from his notes *Life on the Mississippi*

by Colonel Mason

This work is also produced in audio on *iTunes,* and *Amazon Audible* [often free] in living stereo with sound effects, and where the characters seem to come alive. It is historically accurate in content, effects, and mood.
at Amazon Audible: www.riverboatyears.com/col

Copyright 1994 by R. F. Mason in audio form,
Copyright renewed 2019 by R. F. Mason in print and audio.
PO Box 548, Lewisville, TX 75067. 214-329-4949 colonel@prfirm1.com
All rights reserved, no part of this work may be reproduced in any form or by any electronic or mechanical means including information storage and retrieval systems without permission in writing from the copyright holder, except by a reviewer who may quote brief passages in a review.

DEDICATION

To all river pilots down through the ages, past and present, who have bravely navigated our treacherous waters through every conceivable hardship

CONTENTS

1. Introduction
2. In The Beginning
3. Early Boatmen
4. When the Mississippi Flowed Backwards
5. Age of the Steamboat Arrives
6. With Steamboats Came Civilization
7. Ruffians, Outlaws, Harlots, and Thieves
8. Sternwheelers vs. Side-Wheelers
9. River Gamblers
10. Hannibal
11. The Cub Pilot
12. The Leadman
13. Dangerous Chutes
14. Dangerous Snags
15. Gold Rush on the Yukon
16. Steamboat Bill
17. The Pilot was Law
18. The Yazoo River Saved Vicksburg
19. The First Mate

20. Reading the Water
21. Calamities, Wrecks
22. The Majestic River
23. Mark Twain
24. Famous Steamboat Racing
25. Massacre, and the *Far West*
26. Brotherhood of Pilots
27. Dirty River Humor
28. Those Fickle Waters
29. The Great Flood of 1882
30. New Orleans
31. The Mean Captain
32. When River Freight Was King
33. Gradual Demise
34. Excursions, Prohibition, and Liquor
35. License to Pilot More River Than Anyone
36. Epilogue
37. Acknowledgments
38. Index

1. INTRODUCTION

In 1973 I was a news reporter working the St. Louis, Missouri, area on various AM and FM radio stations. Being on the banks of the Mississippi River just below where the Missouri River joins, St. Louis offers history rich in river lore and I gobbled up all I could.

Mark Twain, from Hannibal [just north of St. Louis] was an easy first find, and his *Life on the Mississippi* contributed much to this work. Twain's accounting of the steamboat race to St. Louis from New Orleans between the *Natchez* and *Robert E. Lee* in 1870 is epic. But a Twain contemporary, Steamboat Bill, was also from the area. William Heckmann wrote under the name Steamboat Bill and worked his boats out of a quaint German settlement called Hermann, maybe 70 miles west of St. Louis on the Missouri River.

I loved reading Bill's work, so one sunny afternoon late autumn I drove to Hermann hoping I'd uncover some gem he might have left behind. Amazingly, I barely chanced upon a big one and just before it was lost forever.

In Hermann I discovered a sleepy little village of such character as to have been lifted right out of Bavaria or the Rhineland, now nestled in the foothills of the upper Ozarks on the southern banks of the Missouri. I could see Stone Hill Winery high above the city, known for its labyrinth of arched underground cellars, the largest series in North America. Downtown I spotted a quaint tavern called The Levee House. Thinking that sounded like a great place to start nosing around, I stopped in for a beer. The barkeep was friendly, and I guessed not only because the joint was empty, but maybe Hermann is a naturally welcoming town.

I had hardly downed my first mug when in walks an older, well kept guy, who grabs a stool. "Hi there, Captain Baecker, good to see you again," the barkeep welcomed. Upon hearing *captain* I figured this old guy could be interesting so I introduced myself as a reporter, mentioning my interest in river lore and how I had read the works of Steamboat Bill. He was Kermit Baecker, a riverboat pilot based in Hermann and said he had indeed known Bill Heckmann. "Long gone," Baecker said, "but his brother Ed is still alive, a pilot himself and still here in town."

I leaped off my stool and begged for an introduction. Could Baecker please ask Ed Heckmann of any possibility I could record an interview? Baecker said he'd ask, and to give him a few days to get back to me.

Later that week I met up with Captain Baecker again at the Levee House and he took me to meet Ed Heckmann at his home on a hill overlooking town. The captain greeted us warmly, a tall, straight man with thin white hair the only thing betraying his advanced years. Heckmann's house was neat as a pin. As we sat around his dining table I immediately produced my recorder so as to miss nothing.

"I'm not sure how much help I can be for you," Heckmann began, "my daughter, Dorothy Shrader, plans to write a book. But I'll give you what I can."*

---

*In later years Dorothy Heckmann Shrader did indeed write a book, several of them, all fascinating accounts of her childhood and the Heckmann brothers, especially her uncle Bill. At this writing, these books are still available on Amazon

I recorded close to an hour of candid thoughts from this great relic of a bygone time, captured rich insights and learned what a truly historical figure Ed Heckmann was in being the one person with license to pilot more river than anyone who came before or since.

And I was most lucky to get to him when I did. Ed Heckmann died just a few months after our visit and shortly before his 90th birthday. Over the years I used bits of the Heckmann interview in select radio programs, but not 'till twenty years later did I use the full recording in an audio book released on cassette titled *Those Roaring Riverboat Years*. In that work, as this, I filled in missing pieces with the words of Mark Twain from his book *Life on the Mississippi.*

This book, with the same title as that first on cassette, has been updated, copyright renewed, re-mastered, audio digitized, and now released both in print and audio.

As you read on, you will find Twain and Heckmann often together, since they were indeed contemporaries in life. Plus, since both Twain and Steamboat Bill were river authors, it is not too much a leap to believe they met and had conversations. Did Bill Heckmann bring along his younger brother Ed to visit with Twain? In this book we fancy Ed Heckmann and Mark Twain having that conversation while discussing, of course, the river and a subject they both loved, *reading the water* [see Chapter 20].

This work can be heard in stereo on *iTunes* and *Amazon Audible* where the characters come alive with reenactments of Mark Twain, the actual voice of Ed Heckmann from that long ago interview, and various other character reenactments from the roaring steamboat era.

2. IN THE BEGINNING

Before there could be steamboats, there had to be rivers. And the river system that drains the North American continent is truly spectacular. The Mississippi Basin alone contains about a million square miles, the second great valley of the world, exceeded only by that of the Amazon. And it exceeds in extent the whole of Europe.

Every year it empties four hundred and six million tons of mud into the Gulf of Mexico. Scientists say that the mouth used to be at Baton Rouge. And that two-hundred miles of land between there and the Gulf was built by the river.

3. EARLY BOATMEN

Native Americans learned early this drainage system could be navigated. The Indian word *Missouri*, which now is the name of both a state and a river, means "Canoe Havers."

And then would come the first Europeans, the Spanish. Here is what Mark Twain wrote: "To say that De Soto, the first white man who ever saw the Mississippi River, saw it in 1542 is a remark that states a fact without interpreting it. The date 1542 standing by itself means little or nothing to us. When De Soto took his glimpse of the river, Michelangelo's paint was not yet dry on the Last Judgment in the Sistine Chapel. Mary Queen of Scots was not yet born. The Council of Trent was being called. The Spanish Inquisition was roasting and racking and burning with a free hand. Don Quixote was not yet written. Shakespeare was not yet born. A hundred long years must still elapse before Englishmen would hear the name of Oliver Cromwell."

De Soto merely glimpsed the river, then died, and was buried in it by his priests and soldiers. Twain goes on, " ... when De Soto found it he was not hunting for a river, had no present occasion for one. Consequently he did not value it or take any particular notice of it."

The French came next, but it was no time soon, as Twain wrote: " ... then at last La Salle, the Frenchman, conceived the idea of seeking out that river and exploring it. Why did these people want the river now when nobody had wanted it in the five preceding generations? Apparently, because at this late day, they thought they had discovered a way to make it useful. For it had come to be believed that the Mississippi emptied into the Gulf of California and therefore afforded a shortcut from Canada to China. Previously the supposition had been that it emptied into the Atlantic or the Sea of Virginia.

"In 1673, Louis Jolliet the merchant, and Marquette the priest, crossed the country and reached the banks of the Mississippi. They went by way of the Great Lakes and from Green Bay in canoes. Marquette had solemnly contracted on the Feast of the Immaculate Conception that if the Virgin would permit him to discover the great river he would name it Conception in her honor, and he kept his word."

Marquette had been warned by the Indians that he's on a foolhardy journey, even a fatal one, for "the river contained a demon whose roar could be heard at a great distance, and who would engulf them in the abyss where he dwelt." Marquette writes that he was terrified by a big catfish. And Twain agreed catfish in that river can get huge, "I have seen a Mississippi catfish more than six feet long and weighed 250 pounds, and if Marquette's fish was a fellow to that one he had a fair right to think the river's roaring demon has come." Marquette wrote in his diary that at what is now Alton, Illinois, "a torrent of yellow mud rushed furiously a fourth the calm blue current of the Mississippi, boiling and surging and sweeping in its course, logs, branches and uprooted trees." This was the mouth of the Missouri, "that savage river which, descending from its mad career through a vast unknown of barbarism poured its torpid floods into the bosom of its genteel sister."

River men of later years would agree with Father Marquette about the Missouri River. Famous riverboat pilot, Captain Bill Heckmann, known as *Steamboat Bill*, wrote that "the mouth of the Missouri separated the men from the boys, with the boys staying on the Mississippi."

In Marquette's day a Frenchman could travel by water from New Orleans deep into Canada without leaving French territory. But it was with the emerging United States that the river really became useful, the words of Mark Twain: "… the river's earliest commerce was in great barges, keelboats, broadhorns. They floated and sailed from the upper rivers to New Orleans, changed cargoes there, and were tediously warped and poled back by hand. A voyage down and back sometimes occupied nine months."

4. WHEN THE MISSISSIPPI FLOWED BACKWARDS

In 1811 the lower Mississippi was shaken by a devastating earthquake along the New Madrid Fault. Trappers in the area wrote of seeing the earth pitch and roll, hills and valleys being created right under their feet and before their eyes. The Mississippi River, it is said, actually flowed backwards, and created what is now modern day Reelfoot Lake, Tennessee. As far away as Boston, Massachusetts, dishes rattled in cupboards. If the cities of Memphis and St. Louis were as built up then as they are today, rather than being small trading outposts, they would have been totally destroyed. Nearly the whole of that one-thousand three-hundred miles of that old Mississippi River, which La Salle floated down in his canoes over three-hundred years ago, is good solid ground today.

5. AGE OF THE STEAMBOAT ARRIVES

Ironically, it was that same year, 1811, the first steamboat plied the waters and held so much promise for commerce that traffic flourished by the following year. Mark Twain noted "bye and bye the steamboat intruded. Then for fifteen or twenty years these men continued to run their keelboats downstream and the steamers did all the upstream business; the keel boatmen selling their boats in New Orleans and returning home as deck passengers on the steamers. But after awhile the steamboats so increased in number and speed that they were able to absorb the entire commerce. And then keel boating died a permanent death. The keel boatman became a deckhand or a mate or a pilot on the steamers. And when steamer berths were not open to him he took a berth on a Pittsburg coal flat or on a pine raft constructed in the forests up toward the sources of the Mississippi."

6. WITH STEAMBOATS CAME CIVILIZATION

And the river cities flourished with boats in the water and the people in whiskey. Twain told how the steamboats brought settlers after the whiskey. "This great van leader arrived upon the ground, built the first cabin, uncorked his jug and began to sell whiskey to the Indians. How solemn and beautiful is the thought that the earliest pioneer of civilization, the van leader of civilization, is never the steamboat, never the railroad, never the newspaper, never the Sabbath school, never the missionary, but always whiskey. Such is the case. Look history over, you will see. The missionary comes after the whiskey. I mean he arrives after the whiskey has arrived. Next comes the poor immigrant with axe and hoe and rifle, next the trader. Next the miscellaneous rush, next the gambler, the desperado, the highwaymen, and all their kindred in sin of both sexes. And next, the smart chap who has bought up all the old grant that covers all the land. This brings the lawyer tribe. The Vigilance Committee brings the undertaker. All these interests bring the newspaper. The newspaper starts up politics and a railroad. All hands turn to and build a church and a jail and, behold, civilization is established forever in the land. Westward the jug of influence takes its way."

7. RUFFIANS, OUTLAWS, HARLOTS AND THIEVES

Perhaps the most notorious of these river cities was Natchez, Mississippi, or rather *Natchez Under the Hill*. As reenacted here from old historical accounts the way a river man might have described it. "Natchez ain't no city, no, it's two cities, one high on the bluff and the other low and murky on the river. Us river men never see past the wharf Natchez, ain't good enough. Here the gambler takes our money. If it ain't the gambler, it's the pistol in the dark or a knife in the gullet. We don't always die easy but we die hard. And the evil stench of death and decay eats at you from the dead and dyin'. Streams of waste run from the streets down to the river. We come ashore with a handful of wages and the sharpers rid us of it. After months on the boats all we want is a good time. The whiskey flows, the women dance, it never ends night and day. Here at Natchez Under the Hill is all we want. The women are hard. They look easy, they come on easy. But with these hardened harlots of Natchez you're lucky just to lose your watch and wages, sometimes you can wake up dead. Gamblers, mad drunks, seductive women, dark allies, it's all here.

"But the main street leads up the side of the bluff, and on top of the bluff is the other Natchez, one I never get to see. There Silver Street brings the Natchez of finery, no debauchers there. That's the Natchez *ON* the hill, where gentlemen ply their ladies with the best fineries and subtle glances. Well-dressed slaves cater to any whim. Men bet on great horses. Grand banquets honor the idle rich. And wealthy gentlemen court women with high breeding and strict morals, stately houses, wide lawns, vast plantations, a courthouse, steeple'd churches, acres of slaves to make all this possible, all a life of ease. The children play, dainty women chat and sip fancy drinks. And each fine master, it is said, has a lady in Natchez and another under the hill."

Mark Twain wrote of a typical river man of the day preparing for a fight, "I'm the old original iron-jawed, brass-mounted, copper-bellied corpse-maker from the wilds of Arkansaw!—Look at me! I'm the man they call Sudden Death and General Desolation! Sired by a hurricane, dam'd by an earthquake, half-brother to the cholera, nearly related to the small-pox on the mother's side! Look at me! I take nineteen alligators and a bar'l of whiskey for breakfast when I'm in robust health, and a bushel of rattlesnakes and a dead body when I'm ailing! I split the everlasting rocks with my glance, and I squench the thunder when I speak! Whoo-oop! Stand back and give me room according to my strength! Blood's my natural drink, and the wails of the dyin' is music to my ear! Cast your eye on me, gentlemen!—and lay low and hold your breath, for I'm 'bout to turn myself loose!"

During this period, gangs of virulent desperados infested our lawless frontier waterways. *Cave-in-Rock* cutthroats lured to their deaths unsuspecting travelers off the Ohio River. At their peak, said to be during the 1830s. These human river rats have an epic history of their own, and about whom much has been written.

But Twain chose to tell of a lesser known gang of that time, perhaps the worst. "There is a tradition that Island 37 was one of the principle abiding places of that once celebrated Murrell's gang. This was a colossal combination of robbers, horse thieves, Negro stealers and counterfeiters engaged in business along the river some fifty or sixty years ago.

"While our journey across the country to St. Louis was in progress, we had had no end of Jesse James and his stirring history, for he had just been assassinated by an agent of the governor of Missouri and, of consequence, occupying a good deal of space in the newspapers. Cheap histories of him were for sale by train boys and, according to these he was the most marvelous creature of his kind that had ever existed. It was a mistake. Murrell was his equal in boldness, in pluck, in rapacity, in cruelty, brutality, heartlessness, treachery, and in general, comprehensive vileness and shamelessness, and very much his superior in some larger aspects. James was a retail rascal, Murrell wholesale. James' modest genius dreamed of no loftier flight than the planning of raids upon cars, coaches, and country banks. Murrell projected Negro insurrections and the capture of New Orleans. And furthermore, on occasion, this Murrell could go into a pulpit and edify the congregation. What are James and his half dozen vulgar rascals compared with this stately old time criminal with his sermons, his meditated insurrections, city captures, and his majestic following of ten-hundred men sworn to do his evil will? He appears to have been a most dexterous as well as consummate villain. When he traveled, his usual disguise was that of an itinerant preacher. And it is said that his discourses were very soul moving, interesting to hearers so much that they forgot to look after their horses which were carried away by his confederates while he was preaching.

"But the stealing of horses in one state and selling them in another was but a small portion of their business. The most lucrative was the enticing of slaves to run away from their masters that they might sell them in another quarter. They would tell the Negro that, if he would run away from his mater and allow them to sell him, he should receive a portion of the money paid for him and, upon his return to them a second time, they'd send him to a free state where he would be safe. The poor retches complied with this request hoping to obtain money and freedom. They'd be sold to another master and run away again to their employers. Sometimes they'd be sold in this manner three or four times until they had realized three or four thousand dollars by them. But, as after this there was fear of detection, the usual custom was to get rid of the only witness that could be produced against them, which was the Negro himself, by murdering him."

8. STERNWHEELERS AND SIDE-WHEELERS

This, then, was the heyday of the steamboats, which grew in number but in really only two styles, sternwheelers and side-wheelers. But which is better? To find out we asked the most renowned riverboat pilot of them all, the man who had a license to pilot more river than anyone who had ever lived, and who spoke to me many years ago in 1973, and just a few months short of his death, a brother to Steamboat Bill, the late Captain Ed Heckmann:

"Oh, there's no comparison, they both have their disadvantages and they both have their advantages. Now the side-wheeler, of course, no doubt about being the better maneuver'er for the simple reason … you coming down here with a sternwheeler, and you decide you're going to land in Hermann, you start backing about half a mile above town and when you get pretty near where you want to land then you round-her-to, what we call it, so you run it over and back 'er around. So she has to have about two or three times her own length to turn around, get headed upstream. Whereas your side-wheeler, you can turn her around on a button. You just back one wheel and come ahead on the other and turn around right now. You don't have to have much room.

"But the sternwheeler has a big advantage … we had quite a few nice side-wheelers we didn't have on the Missouri, but a lot of them were sternwheelers. Your side-wheeler is vulnerable when it comes to running into a reef, you know. You may be coming along in nice deep water and a sternwheeler would shear away from it or it wouldn't hurt anything if you run into it sideways. But your old side-wheeler would come along and that wheel would climb out on that reef, you'd liable to have a ruined wheel. And running in the wind your side-wheeler'd have the advantage, but in shallow water the sternwheeler was hard to beat."

OK, so where were the rudders? "Oh, the side-wheeler boat used to have one rudder right in the center. The sternwheeler had two to four, all forward right under the wheel."

9. RIVER GAMBLERS

Steamboats became a Mecca for humanity; gamblers that infested dens such as *Natchez Under the Hill* were run out of more decent communities along the river and found a home on the riverboats, which weren't affected by local community laws. Captain Heckmann remembered: "Well, the gamblers infested the old time packet boats, you know. And nearly all the old packet boats, say on the Mississippi running from New Orleans to St. Louis, there was always one or two gamblers who got aboard some way, come aboard as a passenger and get to mingling with the crew, and then find a couple men who had a little money to lose and get 'em in a gambling game.

10. HANNIBAL

For those who lived along the river the steamboat was magic. Hear the words of Mark Twain: "When I was a boy there was but one permanent ambition among my comrades in our village of Hannibal, Missouri, on the west bank of the Mississippi River. Once a day, a cheap gaudy packet arrived upward from St. Louis, and another downward from Keokuk. Before these events the day was glorious with expectancy. After them the day was a dead and empty thing. Not only the boys, but the whole village felt this.

"After all these years I can picture that old time, myself, now just as it was then. The white town drowsing in the sunshine of a summer's morning, the streets empty, or pretty nearly so. One or two clerks sitting in front of the Water Street stores with their split bottom chairs tilted back against the wall, chins on breasts, hats slouched over their faces, asleep, with shingle shavings enough around to show what broke them down. A sow and a litter of pigs loafing along the sidewalk doing a good business in watermelon rinds and seeds, two or three lonely little freight piles scattered about the levee. A pile of skids on the slope of the stone paved wharf and the fragrant town drunkard asleep in the shadow of them. Two or three wood flats at the head of the wharf, but nobody to listen to the peaceful lapping of the wavelets against them.

"The great Mississippi, the majestic—the magnificent Mississippi, rolling its mile-wide tide along, shining in the sun, the dense forest away on the other side, the point above town and the point below bounding the river glimpse and turning it into a sort of sea, and with all a very still and brilliant and lonely one. Presently, a film of dark smoke appears above one of those remote points. Instantly, a Negro drayman, famous for his quick eye and prodigious voice, lifts up the cry *steamboat's acomin'*, and the scene changes. The town drunkard stirs, the clerks wake up, a furious clatter of drays follows, every house and store pours out a human contribution. All in a twinkling the dead town is alive and moving. Drays, carts, men, boys, all go hurrying from many quarters to a common center. The wharf, assembled there, the people fasten their eyes upon the coming boat as upon a wonder they have seen for the first time. The envy of all, great volumes of the blackest smoke are rolling and tumbling out of the chimneys, a husbanded grandeur created with a bit of pitch pine just before arriving at a town. Then such a scramble there is to get aboard, and to get ashore, and to take in freight, and to discharge freight, all at once and the same time, and such a yelling and cursing. Ten minutes later the steamer is under way again with no flag on the jackstaff and no black smoke issuing from the chimneys. After ten more minutes the town is dead again, and the town drunkard asleep by the skids once more.

"Boy after boy managed to get on the river. So bye and bye I ran away. I said I never would come home until I was a pilot and could come home in glory."

11. THE CUB PILOT

But Mark Twain didn't know then, and would come to know later, that being a pilot meant he had to memorize the entire river, at least the parts he hoped to pilot. And the river was constantly changing. So Twain started out as a pilot's cub and had much to learn. "I supposed that all a pilot had to do was to keep his boat in the river. And I did not consider that to be much of a trick since it was so wide."

They started from New Orleans, upstream, and his chief told him "the easy water was close ashore and the current outside, and therefore we must hug the bank upstream to get the benefit of the former, and stay well out downstream to take advantage of the latter. In my own mind I resolved to be a downstream pilot and leave the up-streaming to people dead to prudence." But he soon learned downstream was more dangerous. "Coming upstream, pilots did not mind low water or any kind of darkness. Nothin' stopped 'em but fog. But downstream work was different. The boat was too nearly helpless with a stiff current pushing her. So it was not customary to run downstream at night or in low water."

12. THE LEADMAN

And when a pilot suspected low water he'd call out the lead's man who would stand on deck dropping a line overboard with a lead weight on the end to tell the depth. Mark three, half twain, mark twain, let's let Captain Heckmann tell us: "Life would get lonesome, they'd get the leadman out to sound water just to hear him sing—mark three, no bottom. Twenty-four feet was no bottom or deep four. Mark twain, … quarter less twain was ten and a half feet, mark twain was twelve feet." Then Captain Heckmann's fellow pilot, Kermit Baecker, added: "They had a sing-song rhythm like, *Three and a Half, a Cow and a Calf.*"

A watch in the pilothouse was four hours on and four off, shared by two pilots and their cubs. At the end of his first watch, Twain went to his quarters, but was rudely awakened from sleep. "Here was something fresh. This getting up in the middle of the night to go to work, it was a detail in piloting that had never occurred to me at all. I knew that boats ran all night but somehow I had never happened to reflect that somebody had to get up out of a warm bed to run them. I began to fear that piloting was not quite so romantic as I had imagined it was. There was something very real and work-like about this new phase of it."

13. DANGEROUS CHUTES

The river current would often eat out narrow channels through land away from the main body of the river. They called these chutes, were often deep enough to navigate, and were reserved for use only of boats going upstream. But they could be treacherous, as Twain said his chief told him. "And mind what I just told you, when you start into one of those places you've got to go through. They are too narrow to turn around in, too crooked to back out of, and the shoal water is always up at the head."

14. DANGEROUS SNAGS

With lack of the communications as we have today, a sudden rise in the water level came with little warning, sometimes just the appearance of more drift coming down before the rise, as Twain wrote. "We met a great rise coming down the river, the whole vast face of the stream was black with drifting dead logs, broken boughs and great trees that had caved in and had been washed away. It required the finest steering to pick one's way through this rushing raft even in the daytime and crossing from point to point, and at night the difficulty was mightily increased. Every now and then a huge log lying deep in the water would suddenly appear right under our bow coming head on. No use to try to avoid it then. We could only stop the engines and one wheel would walk over that log from one end to the other, keeping up a thundering racket and careening the boat in a way that was very uncomfortable to the passengers. Now and then we'd hit one of these sunken logs a rattling bang dead in the center with a full head of steam, and it would stun the boat as if she had hit a continent. Sometimes this log would lodge and stay right across the nose, and back the Mississippi up before it. We'd have to do a little craw fishing then to get away from the obstruction. We'd often hit white logs in the dark for we could not see them until we were right on them, but a black log is a pretty distinct object at night. A white snag is an ugly customer when the daylight is gone.

"Of course, on the great rise down came a swarm of prodigious timber rafts from the headwaters of the Mississippi, coal barges from Pittsburg, little trading scows from everywhere, and broadhorns from Posey County, Indiana, freighted with *Fruit & Furniture*, the usual term for describing it. Though in plain English the freight thus aggrandized was hoop poles and pumpkins. Pilots bore a mortal hatred for these crafts and it was returned with usury.

"The law required all such helpless traders to keep a light burning. But it was a law that was often broken. All of a sudden on a murky night a light would pop up right under our bow almost and an agonized voice with a backwoods wang to it would wail out *where you goin' you blank, blank, blank, one-eyed theivin' son of a bush monkey*. Then for an instant, as we'd whistle by, the red glare from our furnaces would reveal the scow and the form of a gesticulating orator as if under a lightning flash. And in that instant our fireman and deck hands would send and receive a tempest of missiles and profanity. One of our wheels would walk away with the crushing fragments of a steering oar, and down the dead blackness would shut again ... once a coal boatman sent a bullet through our pilothouse when we tore a steering oar off of him in a very narrow place."

So Mark Twain had his adventures going up the current and other trying moments going down: "Piloting is a science when you apply it to vast streams like the Mississippi and the Missouri, whose alluvial banks cave and change constantly, whose snags are always hunting up new quarters, whose sandbars are never at rest, whose channels are forever dodging and shirking, and whose obstruction must be confronted in all nights and all weathers without the aid of a single lighthouse or a single buoy, for there's neither light nor buoy to be found anywhere in all this three or four thousand miles of villainous river. Ship channels are buoyed and lighted and therefore it's a comparatively easy undertaking to learn to run them in the ocean. And clear water rivers with gravel bottoms change their channels very gradually and therefore one needs to learn them but once."

15. GOLD RUSH ON THE YUKON

One of those clear water rivers is the Yukon on which Captain Ed Heckmann was also a pilot as a result of the Klondike Gold Rush near the turn of the 1900's.

"It was so different, there was nothing to worry about like we have on the Missouri. The water of the Yukon, in fact the whole length of the Yukon, changes very, very slowly. Whereas here on the Missouri River, when one of these banks starts to cave in, erode, that sometimes would cut back fifty feet in one day. That bank would just slop in and go on out into the Gulf. Whereas those banks up there are frozen solid, you know, all year with permafrost, and there's no snags to worry about because there's no timber to make a snag, no, nothing large enough to make a troublesome snag, and very few places where you could hit a rock even if you wanted to."

So, easy to navigate gravel-bottom rivers such as the Yukon provide an opportunity for employment for pilots that couldn't make it on the Mississippi or the Missouri.

"Some of those pilots, I don't know where they picked up so many broken down old no-good pilots, but they did from the different rivers, most of them came from the Mississippi, a few of 'em from St. Louis. How they could find so many dumb pilots I don't know, but nearly all those white pilots ... they weren't satisfied unless they had two or three native Indian pilots in the pilothouse with them, and those Indians didn't know anything. We had a young fellow that was a half-breed Russian, mother was a coastal Indian and his daddy had been a Russian, and he'd been educated, pretty well educated. He turned out to be a pretty good pilot."

16. STEAMBOAT BILL

Since we now know piloting a river is so difficult, we asked Captain Heckmann about the comment by his brother, Steamboat Bill, that the men and boys were separated at the mouth of the Missouri.

"In the first place that is a mistake to call the Missouri River *mouth* where the Mississippi enters. The Missouri River is one continuous river from Great Falls, Montana, to New Orleans and the Mississippi is a tributary. Anybody that looks at the map can see that."

Well, he had us on that one. Old rivermen do point out that, where the Missouri and Mississippi join, more water and sediment comes from the Missouri and therefore should be called the Missouri River all the way to New Orleans. But that still didn't answer the real question: Is the Missouri harder to navigate than the upper reaches of the Mississippi?

"Now those were all wooden hull boats. From St. Louis to St. Paul, nine-hundred miles, before we had any locks. I mean that was just winding around, you go around a rock dyke here and around a rock point here, and you wind your way … and they'd run those boats at night. And I consider that some of the best piloting that was ever done on any river. So that was all a very foolish remark for Bill to make. But there's no comparison, it's just two different kinds of steamboating altogether. As a Mississippi pilot, after you once do the river, it was fixed in your mind because it wasn't constantly shifting. But the Missouri was shifting every few hours. You may come up and go by Hermann this side this week and come back down in ten days in a channel the other side of the river. That kind of change, you know."

17. THE PILOT WAS LAW

The words of Mark Twain tell us how independent a creature a pilot really was, " … a pilot in those days was the only unfettered and entirely independent human being that lived in the Earth. The captain could stand upon the Hurricane Deck in the pomp of a very brief authority and give him five or six orders. Until the vessel backed into the stream, and then that skipper's reign was over. The moment that the boat was under way in the river she was under the sole and unquestioned control of the pilot. He could do with her exactly as he pleased. Run her when and whither he chose. And tie her up to the bank whenever his judgment said that course was best. His movements were entirely free, he consulted no one, he received commands from nobody, and he promptly resented even the merest suggestions."

Absolute power? Captain Heckmann agreed. "Well that's right, the minute you leave the shore you have a law of your own, you know, you don't have to comply with any shore laws. The master of the boat has the same authority as a marshal would have on shore when you're under way. So you don't have to worry about it, if you want to arrest a man away from shore you can do so."

But with this power came terrible responsibilities. A pilot can never leave his post, as Twain wrote, " … the cub pilot is early admonished to despise all perils connected with a pilot's calling, and to prefer any sort of death to the deep dishonor of deserting his post. The history of piloting affords six or seven instances of this sort of martyrdom, and a half hundred instances of escape from a like fate which came within a second or two of being fatally too late. But there is no instance of a pilot deserting his post to save his life whereby, remaining and sacrificing it, he might secure other lives from destruction. Several others whom I had known had fallen in the war. One or two of them shot down at the wheel."

Mark Twain was referring, of course, to the Civil War, which practically shut down all riverboat traffic for a time, causing a number of pilots to die under fire and others to seek another line of work, Mark Twain included.

18. THE YAZOO RIVER SAVED VICKSBURG

Nowhere was the problem more acute for steamboats than at Vicksburg, Mississippi, below the bluff of which the Mississippi

River makes a wide looping turn as it is joined by the Yazoo River and creates a fingerlike peninsula out of a strip of Louisiana. This strategic location gave the batteries at Vicksburg absolute command of the river at that point. As early as 1861 all steamers passing Vicksburg were stopped for examination. Union forces couldn't tolerate this but were powerless to stop it. Harper's *History of the Great Rebellion* wrote at the time, "Vicksburg, which as regards to heroic and obstinate to the national arms, held almost equal rank with Richmond and Charleston. It is the most important, and at the same time, the most defensible military position on the Mississippi."

By 1863 the only steamboats able to pass Vicksburg were ocean-going class military gun boats. Riverboat commerce had largely come to an end. In a clever attempt to bypass Vicksburg altogether, Union forces engaged hundreds of freed slaves to cut a canal across that narrow strip of Louisiana and drive Vicksburg six miles inland. By 1863 all such attempts had failed, most surely because a healthy current from the Yazoo River, spilling into the Mississippi from the east bank just above Vicksburg, kept that main channel open. General Grant then settled in for a long siege of the city. So if not for the Yazoo River, Vicksburg might well have been landlocked to this day.

After the war, former slaves enjoyed moving around at will, since previously they hadn't been allowed to do so. And for those along the river a favorite choice was flagging down a steamboat, as Twain reported:

"Sometimes there was a single lonely landing cabin. Near it, the colored family that had hailed us, little and big, old and young, roosting on a scant pile of household goods, these consisting of a rusty gun, some bed ticks, chests, chim ware, stools, a crippled looking-glass, a venerable arm chair, and six or eight baseborn and spiritless yellow curs attached to the family by strings. They must have their dogs, can't go without their dogs. But the dogs are never willing, they always object. So one after another in ridiculous procession they're dragged aboard, all four feet braced and sliding along the stage, head likely to be pulled off but the tugger marching determinedly forward, bending to his work with the rope upon his shoulder for better purchase. Sometimes a child is forgotten and left on the bank but never a dog."

19. THE FIRST MATE

So the pilot is king and the captain sets policy, but it's the First Mate that makes things happen. Mark Twain described his very first First Mate. "When he gave even the very simplest order he discharged it like a blast of lightning. He sent a long reverberating peel of profanity thundering after it. I could not help contrasting the way in which the average landsman would give an order with the mate's way of doing it. If the landsman should wish the gangplank moved a foot farther forward he would probably say: *James, or William, ah one of you, push that plank forward please.* But put the Mate in his place and he would roar out: '**Here now, set that gangplank forward! Blimey now, what you're about, snatch it—snatch it, there—there, aft again—aft again. Don't you hear me? Dash it to dash, are you goin' to sleep over it? Vast heavin', vast heavin' I tell you, goin' to heave it clear astern! Where you goin' with that barrel? Forward with it 'for I make ya swallow it, you dash, dash, dash split between a tired mud turtle and a crippled hearse horse.**' I wished I could talk like that."

20. READING THE WATER

A remarkable skill that pilots had to acquire was *reading the water*. Hear the words of Mark Twain and the voice of Captain Ed Heckmann, as though in conversation about it.

Heckmann first would say "It's a talent you have to develop. I don't know, I guess some people are born with it. And some men work on the river all their life and don't know. You have to know what we call *reading the water*, you hafta … by looking at the surface of the water you hafta tell … every little ripple tells you something."

And then Twain would add: "I had often seen pilots gazing at the water and pretending to read it as if it were a book. A book that was a dead language to the uneducated passenger, but which told its mind to me without reserve, delivering its most cherished secrets as clearly as if it uttered them with a voice. And it was not a book that was to be read once and thrown aside, for it had a new story to tell every day. There is a bar under every point because the water that comes down around it forms an eddy and allows the sediment to sink."

That's when Heckmann would speak up again. "Different types of obstructions will make a different kind, of what we call, a break on the water…"

And then Twain would step in to agree, "…and the fine lines on the face of the water, that branch out like the ribs of a fan, those are little reefs…"

And Heckmann would quickly add: " ... and there's all kinds of little tricks too, for learning to read the reefs, you know. And the surface of the water is never the same, ya know, never two days alike."

Twain quickly adds, "You can see the difference. There's a wind reef, the wind does it but it's exactly like a bluff reef, and how to tell them apart I can't tell ya. It's an instinct. Bye and bye you just naturally know one from the other. But you never will be able to explain why, or how you know them apart ..."

On that, Heckmann jumps in, "... you learn that by actual sight and if you don't have that sixth sense I don't think you ever learn it."

Twain readily agrees, "You see this has got to be learned. A clear starlit night throws such heavy shadows that if you didn't know the shape of a shore perfectly you would claw away from every bunch of timbers 'cause you would take the black shadow of it for a solid cape. You'd be fifty yard away from shore every time when you ought to be fifty feet of it..."

And then Heckmann remembers "I've been around men on the river for years and never learned anything, and some fellows pick up ... come right in off a farm and first thing ya know they're first class pilots. They just have that peculiar talent you have to have, the talent of knowing how to read the water, and you have to have an awful lot of self confidence. That's among the main things, and a very good memory."

But Twain countered that memory is no good when you can't see. "Then there's your pitch dark night. The river is a very different shape on a pitch dark night from what it is on a starlit night. Then there's your gray mist. You take a night when there is one of those grisly, drizzly gray mists and then there isn't any particular shape to a shore. A gray mist would tangle the head of the oldest man that ever lived."

Heckmann quickly agreed, " … if you have a little rainy spell, a little rain on the water you just as well forget about your knowledge of reading water because it can't be done. But that usually just lasts for a short time."

Then Twain remembered " … a passenger who could not read the water was charmed with a peculiar sort of faint dimple on its surface, on the rare occasions when he did not overlook it altogether. But to the pilot, that was an italicized passage. Indeed, it was more than that, it was a legend of the largest capitals with a string of shouting exclamation at the end of it for it meant that a wreck, or a rock, was buried there that could tear the life out of the strongest vessel that ever floated. It is the faintest and simplest expression the water ever makes, and the most hideous to a pilot."

So Heckmann added " … the river looks different going upstream than it does coming downstream. It is all something that has to be acquired and, as I say, I think it is some sort of sixth sense that you're born with."

Twain agreed, and said " … after I learned to read the water I lost something which could never be restored to me while I lived. All the grace, the beauty, the poetry had gone out of the majestic river. I began to cease from noting the glories and charms. The sun means that we're going to have wind tomorrow. That floating log means that the river is rising, small thanks to it. That slanting mark on the water refers to a bluff reef which is going to kill somebody's steamboat one of these nights if it keeps on stretching out like that. Those tumbling boils show a dissolving bar and a changing channel there. The lines and the circles in the slick water over yonder are a warning that the troublesome place is shoaling up dangerously. That silver streak in the shadow of the forest is a break from a new snag, and he's located himself in the very best place he could have found to fish for steamboats. That tall dead tree with a single living branch, not going to last long; and then how is a body ever going to get through this blind place at night without the friendly old landmark."

That reminded Heckmann of his days when Indians were used in his pilothouse: "An Indian knew landmarks, you know. If he once saw a place he'd remember. But he never learned to read water. That was beyond his comprehension."

21. CALAMITIES, WRECKS

With the rivers this treacherous we're not surprised hearing about mighty wrecks, and Captain Heckmann said floating logs were most often the cause. "Oh, snags was your... I'd say about at least eighty percent of the boats sunk on the Missouri River were sunk by snags."

Captain Heckman's brother, Steamboat Bill, had written "whiskey sunk most of them," so I asked Ed Heckmann about collisions: "It has happened numerous times on the Ohio River, they've had terrific collisions where two big side-wheelers got confused about their signals, went together, and probably usually in a case of that kind the first thing that happens is a fire and they were destroyed by fire. They've had some terrible calamities on the Ohio River, but very seldom on the Mississippi. But on the Ohio it has happened numerous cases. I don't remember hearing of one on the Missouri."

Often the worst catastrophes were not from collisions but when steam boilers blew up in the days before laws regulated how much pressure was allowed. Mark Twain wrote how his younger brother, Henry, died.

"It was six o'clock on a hot summer morning. The *Pennsylvania* was creeping along, north of Ship Island, about sixty miles below Memphis on a half-head of steam, towing a wood-flat which was fast being emptied. George Ealer was in the pilot-house—alone, I think; the second engineer and a striker had the watch in the engine room; the second mate had the watch on deck; George Black, Mr. Wood, and my brother, clerks, were asleep, as were also Brown and the head engineer, the carpenter, the chief mate, and one striker; Captain Klinefelter was in the barber's chair, and the barber was preparing to shave him. There were a good many cabin passengers aboard and three or four hundred deck passengers—so it was said at the time—and not very many of them were astir. The wood being nearly all out of the flat now, Ealer rang to 'come ahead' full steam, and the next moment four of the eight boilers exploded with a thunderous crash, and the whole forward third of the boat was hoisted toward the sky! The main part of the mass, with the chimneys, dropped upon the boat again, a mountain of riddled and chaotic rubbish—and then, after a little, fire broke out.

"Many people were flung to considerable distances and fell in the river; among these were Mr. Wood and my brother, and the carpenter. The carpenter was still stretched upon his mattress when he struck the water seventy-five feet from the boat. Brown, the pilot, and George Black, chief clerk, were never seen or heard of after the explosion. The barber's chair, with Captain Klinefelter in it and unhurt, was left with its back overhanging vacancy—everything forward of it, floor and all, had disappeared; and the stupefied barber, who was also unhurt, stood with one toe projecting over space, still stirring his lather unconsciously and saying not a word.

"When George Ealer saw the chimneys plunging aloft in front of him, he knew what the matter was; so he muffled his face in the lapels of his coat, and pressed both hands there tightly to keep this protection in its place so that no steam could get to his nose or mouth. He had ample time to attend to these details while he was going up and returning. He presently landed on top of the unexploded boilers, forty feet below the former pilot-house, accompanied by his wheel and a rain of other stuff, and enveloped in a cloud of scalding steam. All of the many who breathed that steam died; none escaped. But Ealer breathed none of it. He made his way to the free air as quickly as he could; and when the steam cleared away he returned and climbed up on the boilers again, and patiently hunted out each and every one of his chessmen and the several joints of his flute.

"By this time the fire was beginning to threaten. Shrieks and groans filled the air. A great many persons had been scalded, a great many crippled; the explosion had driven an iron crowbar through one man's body—I think they said he was a priest. He did not die at once, and his sufferings were very dreadful. A young French naval cadet of fifteen, son of a French admiral, was fearfully scalded, but bore his tortures manfully. Both Mates were badly scalded, but they stood to their posts, nevertheless. They drew the wood-boat aft, and they and the captain fought back the frantic herd of frightened immigrants till the wounded could be brought there and placed in safety first.

"When Mr. Wood and Henry fell in the water, they struck out for shore, which was only a few hundred yards away; but Henry presently said he believed he was not hurt (what an unaccountable error!), and therefore would swim back to the boat and help save the wounded. So they parted, and Henry returned.

"By this time the fire was making fierce headway, and several persons who were imprisoned under the ruins were begging piteously for help. All efforts to conquer the fire proved fruitless; so the buckets were presently thrown aside and the officers fell-to with axes and tried to cut the prisoners out. A striker was one of the captives; he said he was not injured, but could not free himself; and when he saw that the fire was likely to drive away the workers, he begged that someone would shoot him, and thus save him from the more dreadful death. The fire did drive the axmen away, and they had to listen, helpless, to this poor fellow's supplications 'till the flames ended his miseries.

"The fire drove all into the wood-flat that could be accommodated there; it was cut adrift then, and it and the burning steamer floated down the river toward Ship Island. They moored the flat at the head of the island, and there, unsheltered from the blazing sun, the half-naked occupants had to remain, without food or stimulants, or help for their hurts, during the rest of the day. A steamer came along, finally, and carried the unfortunates to Memphis, and there the most lavish assistance was at once forthcoming. By this time Henry was insensible. The physicians examined his injuries and saw that they were fatal, and naturally turned their main attention to patients who could be saved.

"Forty of the wounded were placed upon pallets on the floor of a great public hall, and among these was Henry. There the ladies of Memphis came every day with flowers, fruits, and dainties, and delicacies of all kinds, and there they remained and nursed the wounded. All the physicians stood watches there, and all the medical students; and the rest of the town furnished money, or whatever else was wanted. And Memphis knew how to do all these things well; for many a disaster like the *Pennsylvania*'s had happened near her doors, and she was experienced, above all other cities on the river, in the gracious office of the Good Samaritan'

"The sight I saw when I entered that large hall was new and strange to me, two long rows of prostrate forms—more than forty in all—and every face and head a shapeless wad of loose raw cotton. It was a gruesome spectacle."

22. THE MAJESTIC RIVER

Mark Twain and his brother had had a very close relationship, with a conversation only the previous day how each would be sure to stay at his post in trouble or accident. His brother dying on the river made the waters even more solemn for him as, after establishing himself as a writer, Twain went back to the river as a passenger in 1882.

"I had myself called with the four o'clock watch, mornings, for one cannot see too many summer sunrises on the Mississippi. They are enchanting. First, there is the eloquence of silence, for a deep hush broods everywhere. Next, there's the haunting sense of loneliness, isolation, remoteness from the worry and bustle of the world. The dawn creeps in stealthily. The solid walls of black forest soften to gray. Vast stretches of the river open up and reveal themselves. The water is glade smooth, gives off a spectral little wreath of white mist. There is not the faintest breath of wind nor stir of leaf. The tranquility is profound and infinitely satisfying.

"Then a bird pipes up. Another follows, and soon the piping develops into a jubilant riot of music. You see none of the birds, you simply move through an atmosphere of song which seems to sing itself. When the light has become a little stronger, you have one of the fairest and softest pictures imaginable. You have the intense green of amassed and crowded foliage nearby. You see it paling shade by shade in front of you upon the next projecting cape a mile off or more. The tint is like root of the tender young green of spring. The cape beyond that one has almost lost its color, and the farthest one, miles away under the horizon, sleeps upon the water a mere dim vapor, and hardly separable from the sky above it and about it.

"And all this stretch of river is a mirror. And you have the shadowy reflections of the leafage and the curving shore and the receding capes pictured in it. Well, that is all beautiful, soft and rich and beautiful. And when the sun gets well up and distributes a faint flush here and a powder of gold yonder and a purple haze where it will yield the best effect, ya grant that you have seen something that is worth remembering."

23. MARK TWAIN

Samuel Langhorne Clemens, born 1835—died 1910, perhaps the most gifted of American writers, certainly the most celebrated. But how did he get his pen name, Mark Twain, what he called his *nom de guerre*, or French for *war name*? You only think you know. Hear the words of the man himself:

"It was from Captain Isaiah Sellers.* The old gentleman was not of literary turn or capacity, but he used to jot down brief paragraphs of plain practical information about the river, and sign them Mark Twain, and give them to the New Orleans Picayune. They related to the stage and condition of the river, and were accurate and valuable, and thus far they contained no poison. But in speaking of the stage of the river today, at a given point the captain was pretty apt to drop

---

*Capt. Isaiah Sellers, 1802—1864. His grave and headstone can be found in Bellefontaine Cemetery, St. Louis, Missouri

in a little remark about his being the first time he'd ever seen water so high, or so low, at that

particular point, for 49 years or so, and then, now and then he'd mention island so and so and follow it in parenthesis with some such observation as 'disappeared in 1807 if I remember rightly.' And in these antique interjections lay poison and bitterness for the other old pilots. And they used to chaff the Mark Twain paragraphs with unsparing mockery.

"It so chanced that one of these paragraphs became the text for my first newspaper article. I burlesqued it broadly, very broadly, stringing my fantasies out to the extent of eight-hundred or a thousand words. I was a cub at the time. I showed my performance to some pilots and they eagerly rushed into print in the New Orleans True Delta. It was a great pity because it did nobody any worthy service, and it sent a deep pang into a good man's heart.

"There was no malice in my rubbish, but it laughed at the Captain. It laughed at a man to whom such a thing was new and strange and dreadful. I did not know then, though I do know now, that there is no suffering comparable with that which a private person feels when he is, for the first time, pilloried in print.

"Captain Sellers did me the honor to profoundly detest me from that day forth. It was a very real honor to be in the thoughts of so great a man as Captain Sellers. It was a distinction to be loved by such a man. But it was a much greater distinction to be hated by him, because he loved scores of people, but he didn't sit up nights to hate anybody but me.

"He never printed another paragraph while he lived. And he never again signed Mark Twain to anything. At the time that the telegraph brought the news of his death I was on the Pacific coast. I was a fresh new journalist and needed a nom de guerre so I confiscated the ancient mariner's discarded one. And I have done my best to make it ... remain the petrified truth."

24. FAMOUS STEAMBOAT RACING

With the rivers so dangerous we might think speed wasn't important. But the old rivermen took pride in running their boats and speed was a part of it. Mark Twain writes how racing was sport:

"In the old times, whenever two fast boats started out on a race with a big crowd of people looking on, it was inspiring to hear the crews sing, especially if the times were nightfall and the forecastle lit up with the red glare of the torch basket.

"Racing was royal fun. The people always had an idea that racing was dangerous, for as the opposite was the case, that is, after the laws were passed which restricted each boat to just so many pounds of steam to the square inch. No engineer was ever sleepy or careless when his heart was in a race. He was constantly on the alert, trying gauge cocks and watching things. The dangerous place was on slow plodding boats where the engineers drowsed around and allowed chips to get into the doctor and shut of the water supply from the boilers.

"In the flush times of steamboating, a race between two notoriously fleet steamers was an event of vast importance. The date was set for it several weeks in advance. And from that time forward the whole Mississippi Valley was in a state of consuming excitement. Politics and the weather were dropped, and people talked only of the coming race.

"As the time approached, the two steamers stripped and got ready. Every encumbrance that added weight or exposed a resisting surface to wind or water was removed if the boat could possibly do without it. The spars, and sometimes even their supporting derricks, were sent ashore. And no means left to set the boat afloat in case she got aground. If the boat was known to make her best speed when drawing five and a half feet forward and five feet aft, she was carefully loaded to that exact figure. Hardly any passengers were taken because they not only added weight, but they never will trim boat. They always run to the side when there's something to see, whereas a conscientious and experienced steamboatman would stick to the center of the boat and part his hair in the middle with a spirit level. No way-freights and no way-passengers were allowed, for the racers would stop only at the largest towns. Then it would only be touch and go. Coal flats and wood flats were contracted for beforehand. And these were kept ready to hitch onto the flying steamers at a moment's warning. Double crews were carried so that all work could be quickly done.

"The chosen date being come, and all things in readiness, the two great steamers backed into the stream, lie there and jogging in the moment, apparently watching each other's slightest movement, flags drooping, the spent steam shrieking through safety valves, the black smoke rolling and tumbling from the chimneys and darkening all the air. People, people everywhere, the shores, the housetops, the steamboats, the ships are packed with them. And you know that the borders of the broad Mississippi are going to be fringed with humanity thence northward for twelve-hundred miles to welcome these racers. Presently, tall columns of steam bursts from the escape pipes of both steamers. Two guns boom a goodbye. Two red-shirted heroes mounted on capstans wave their small flags above the mass crews on the forecastle. Two plaintive solos linger in the air, and within seconds, two mighty choruses burst forth and … here they come. Brass bands bray *Hail Columbia*, huzza after huzza thundering from the shores and the stately creatures go whistling by like the wind. Two hot steamboats, raging along, neck and neck, straining every nerve, that is to say every rivet in the boilers, quaking and shaking and groaning from stem to stern, spouting white steam from the pipes, pouring black smoke from the chimneys, raining down sparks, parting the river into long breaks of hissing foam. This is sport! And it's sport that makes a body's very liver curl with enjoyment.

"Those boats will never halt a moment between New Orleans and St. Louis except for a second or two at large towns where they hitch 30-cord wood boats alongside. You should be onboard when they take a couple of those wood boats in tow and turn a swarm of men into each. By the time you wiped your glasses and put them on you'll be wondering what had become of that wood?

"Two nicely matched steamers will stay in sight of each other day after day. They might even stay side by side but for the fact that pilots are not all alike, and the smartest pilot will win the race. If one of the boats has a lightening pilot whose partner is a trifle his inferior, you can tell which one's on watch by noting whether the boat is gaining ground or lost some during each four hour stretch. The shrewdest pilot can delay a boat if he is not a fine genius for steering. Steering is a very high art. One must not keep a rudder dragging across a boats stern if he wants to get up the river fast. The time made by the *Robert E. Lee* from New Orleans to St. Louis in 1870, in her famous race with the *Natchez*, is the best on record. The *Lee* left New Orleans Thursday, June 30, 1870, at four o'clock and fifty-five minutes P.M., and landed at St. Louis at eleven twenty-five A.M. on July fourth, 1870, six hours and thirty-six minutes ahead of the *Natchez*."

25. MASSACRE, and the *FAR WEST*

Well, the *Robert E. Lee* over the *Natchez* might well have been the best time in a steamboat race, but another steamboat six years after that had a race with death on the Missouri and broke speed records that have not been beaten to this day, about double what the *Robert E. Lee* did. After the Custer massacre at the Little Bighorn, the steamer *Far West* carried the news and wounded soldiers of Major Reno and Capt. Benteen's command to civilization. We know exactly what happened from detailed accounts of the time. Hear a reenactment of the tale as though told by one of the cavalrymen badly wounded near the Custer massacre and brought to civilization on the *Far West*.

"Yeh, that boat saved my life and a heap of my fellows. I was with Capt. Benteen, pinned down under the hills near the Little Bighorn. We figured Custer's detachment had been wiped out because we met some stiff fightin' from an ocean of Injuns, and Major Reno and his men were accounted for, but Custer not. I got shot clean through when I went for water for the wounded. All we had were those dern Army issued single-shot 45-70s. The Injuns had traded with gunrunners and the lead they threw at us came from their new Winchester repeaters.

"My wounds didn't finish me off right away, but would have if I didn't get in a hurry to the Army medics in Bismarck. Fifty-two of us were badly shot up. Lucky we had that boat. We hadn't figured to need it for this. Captain Grant Marsh had done what no other pilot had ever done. He had nosed his big steamboat up the Little Bighorn mouth to be as near Custer as possible with supplies and ammunition. That Crow scout, Curly, whose Indian name Ashishishe none of us could pronounce, had been loaned to Custer by Gen. Gibbon and had escaped from the battlefield before the fight had started. He knew it was gonna be a hard scrape but he carried news of the Custer wipeout to the Far West, lightnin'. That way, Captain Marsh was ready for us when the others carried us down to the boat, some many miles, in hand litters. Two days after I ate that lead he had the boat wooded up and grass cut along the banks to pad the decks so we could lie on it. Gen. Terry and Gen. Gibbon told Captain Marsh to take us down river as soon as possible so our wounds could get fixed and news could be telegraphed back East.

"When the sun comes up on the 30th of June, Captain Grant Marsh signals the go-ahead. He shares the pilot duties with Dave Campbell, and Mate Ben Thompson is second in command. Just as important was engineer George Faulk who had to keep tight rein on the levers. These were the bravest, pluckiest men I'd ever met, and we wounded troopers were grateful to God for all of 'em for it was more than skill and navigation needed on this trip, but the luck of Providence had to be with us too.

"Marsh solemnly took his duty, knowing the danger ahead before all of us. The river was loaded with terrible snags, sand bars that could break us in two or strand us 'till the rainy season, and other dire obstacles at every curve. It's hard to be over nine-hundred miles away from the closest civilization, that's how long this river trip was gonna be. 'Cause in June of 1876, this land is unknown as the

Amazon jungles. The Little Bighorn is about the width of a good-size creek. We had to take it to the Bighorn which ain't much better, thence to the Yellowstone which winds its way to the Missouri where the goin' really gets treacherous.

"Captain Marsh demanded and got a full head of steam, what he called 'the very limit of safety.' I remember clean as cheap whiskey that first fifty-three miles down the Bighorn where she emptied into the Yellowstone. Dodgin' round them islands was fancy work since the captain had only seen the channel once before on the up-trip. It was narrow, but we made it.

"On the weekend of July 3rd we headed down the Yellowstone. I don't know of which I was more scared, of tyin' up for the night and not getting' to the dock in time, or runnin' at night, which no boat had ever done, because it would be a dern sight lucky to ever see mornin'. But Captain Marsh told us 'there'd be no tyin' up, we'd run day and night 'till we got there, or go to the devil tryin'.

"I remember years later the other old rivermen talkin' about it, like Captain Ed Heckman: 'The boats going up the mountain did very little night running, don't see how they could. They didn't have a searchlight, and how in the world would you find a snag on a dark night?' We sure didn't know it at the time, but rivermen would be talkin' about this run well into the next century.

"What a wild race with death, the steam-gauge always at the danger mark, or just below it. I never saw a thing like it as we raced down that channel. One way we're lucky 'cause the Yellowstone was carrin' a high rise of water. But in another way that was unlucky, 'cause snags come in high supply and the river is always full of drift. Captain Marsh had set the pace and the crew kept her turnin'. Below the boiler deck those poor grimy firemen fed the wood night and day without much in the way of rest; 'cause not one of us expected we'd ever hafta run like this, and the crew was too light for it. I swore then, if I ever got back to Youngstown, Ohio, alive, I'd never leave it again for nothin'.

"The boat rattled and quaked from the terrible strain we were puttin' on it. Every time we hit a snag the boat groaned and pitched so bad I thought it was curtains. I cain't tell ya how many times we scraped a bank and crossin' a bar. Why that river didn't come in and drown us all I cain't tell ya. Only that by now I've learned that Captain Marsh and his crew were the bravest and best rivermen I'd ever seen. We musta been a sight, every time the captain tooted that whistle we'd send whole herds of buffalo on stampede.

"We finally made the Missouri, and made a stop at Fort Buford there for just the quickest moment to land a wounded Injun scout that wasn't gonna last to Bismarck. Folks who crowded with questions heard scant answers as we shoved off again for the wild ride down the Missouri. By Fort Stevenson, Captain Marsh had draped the jackstaff in black to honor the dead and wounded.

"The Missouri was a lot worse than the Yellowstone, I mean with snags and shifting channels and all. The scare was so great I quit worrin' 'bout my wounds, thinkin' I'd die first from heart failure.

"On July fifth, at nearly 11 o'clock at night, the wharf at Bismarck made a fine welcome sight, and we no sooner moored up than the crew ran through the town spreadin' the news. Everyone was sleepin' but they roused the newspaper editor and the telegraph operator who then had to stay awake for twenty-two hours sendin' the terrible news to the rest of civilization.

"When we counted up all, we were amazed to find out the *Far West* had done somethin' never before done or since, runnin' nearly one thousand miles of dangerous river in just fifty-four hours. This set Captain Marsh, his crew and his boat, in a special place forever in riverboat history."

Of course it did. And Captain Ed Heckmann, who was born just a few years afterward, told me in 1973 "those pilots that were able to take a boat up the Missouri river, from St. Louis to Fort Benton, which is twenty-two hundred and eighty miles, on a treacherous river with no markings whatever, no lights, no channel buoys, no nothin'! And you picked your own channel because the channel is constantly shifting. And I consider that those pilots were remarkable men."

26. BROTHERHOOD OF PILOTS

And so they were "remarkable men," and they enjoyed a mutual respect and brotherhood between them, as Mark Twain wrote of his first trip in the pilothouse heading downstream: "The pilothouse was full of pilots going down to look at the river. What is called the *upper river*, the two-hundred miles between St. Louis and Cairo, Illinois, where the Ohio comes in. And it was low. And the Mississippi changes its channels so constantly that the pilots used to always find it necessary to run down to Cairo to take a fresh look when their boats were to lie in port a week, that is, when the water was at a low stage. A deal of this 'looking at the river' was done by poor fellows who seldom had a berth. Whose only hope of getting one lay with their being freshly posted and therefore ready to drop into the shoes of some reputable pilot for a single trip on account of such pilot's sudden illness or some other necessity. And a good many of them constantly ran up and down inspecting the river. Not because they ever really hoped to get a berth but, because they being guests of the boat, it was cheaper to look at the river than to stay ashore and pay board.

"In time, these fellows grew dainty in their tastes and only infested boats that had an established reputation for setting good tables. All visiting pilots were useful. For they were always ready and willing, winter or summer, night or day, to go out in the yawl and help buoy the channel or assist the boat's pilots in any way they could. They were likewise welcome aboard because all pilots are tireless talkers when gathered together, and they talk only about the river. They're always understood and they're always interesting. They'd say something like, 'Jim, how did ya run Plumb Point comin' up?' And he'd reply, 'well, it was at night there and I ran it the way one of the boys on the Dianna told me. Started out about fifty yards above the wood pile on the false point, and held on the cabin under Plum Point 'till I raised the reef, quarter less twain, and then straightened for the middle bar 'till I got abreast of the old one-limbed cottonwood in the bend. And got my stern on the cottonwood, and head on the bow placed above the point, and came through a-boomin', nine and a half.' And he'd say, 'pretty square crossin', ain't it? And he'd reply, 'yeah, but the upper bat's workin' down fast.'

"Your true pilot cares nothing about anything on earth but the river. His pride in his occupation surpasses the pride of kings."

27. DIRTY RIVER HUMOR

Constant jokes were told about the muddiness of the Missouri River. Farmers along the river say they can make their grindstones by running the water through a hollow log and sawing it off in slices as it comes out the other end.

Mark Twain wrote "I could drink it if I had some other water to wash it down with. It comes out of the turbulent, bank-caving Missouri. And every tumbler full of it holds nearly an acre of land in solution. If you'll let your glass stand half an hour you can separate the land from the water as easy as Genesis. Then you'll find them both good. But the natives do not take them separately, but together as nature mixed them. When they find an inch of mud in the bottom of a glass they stir it up and take the draft as they would gruel."

Of course, to power the steamboats, wood and coal had to be constantly brought aboard, while there is a steady supply of water for the steam boilers from the river itself. But when that river water is dense with mud it's no good for the boilers. So water for the boilers is taken from the top of the water collected while the sediment is allowed to fall and collect at bottom. When the bottom reservoir is loaded with mud it's then dumped back into the river, which makes quite a racket and shivers the boat.

Twain wrote that an Irishman in St. Louis once told him he didn't drink it, that an Irishman won't even drink beer: "They don't drink it, Sir. They can't drink it sir. Give an Irishman lager for once and he's a dead man. An Irishman is lined with copper and the beer corrodes it, sir. But whiskey, oh, whiskey polishes the copper and it's the saving of him, sir."

28. THOSE FICKLE WATERS

Yes, there are a lot of jokes about the muddy water. Old timers used to say the river is 'just and equitable. It never tumbles one man's farm overboard without building a new farm just like it for that man's neighbor. This keeps down hard feelings.'

But in reality, the jokes just softened the many tragedies of living near a savage river, the words of Mark Twain: "By cutting through narrow necks of land, the river straightens and shortens itself. More than once it has shortened itself thirty miles at a single jump. These cutoffs have curious affects that have thrown several river towns into the rural districts and built up sand bars and forests in front of them. A cutoff plays havoc with boundary lines and jurisdictions. For instance, a man living in the state of Mississippi today, a cutoff occurs tonight, and tomorrow the man finds himself and his land over on the other side of the river, within the boundaries of, and subject to the laws of the state of Louisiana. Such a thing happening in the upper river in the old times could have transferred a slave from Missouri to Illinois and made a free man of him.

"When the state of Arkansas was chartered she controlled to the center of the river, a most unstable line. The state of Mississippi claimed to the channel, another shifty and unstable line. Island number 74 belonged to Arkansas. Bye and bye a cutoff threw this big island out of Arkansas, and yet not within Mississippi … middle of the river on one side of it, channel on the other. That is, as I understand the problem. Whether I got the details right or wrong, this fact remains. That here is this big and exceedingly valuable island of four thousand acres thrust out in the cold and belonging to neither the one state nor the other, paying taxes to neither, owing allegiance to neither. One man owns the whole island and, in right, is a man without a country.

"Island 92 belonged to Arkansas. The river moved it over and joined it to Mississippi. A chap established a whiskey shop there without a Mississippi license and enriched himself upon Mississippi custom under Arkansas protection. For no license, in those days, was required.

"When the river is rising fast, some scoundrel whose plantation is back in the country and therefore of inferior value, has only to watch his chance, cut a little gutter across the narrow neck of land some dark night and turn the water into it. And in a wonderfully short time a miracle has happened. The whole Mississippi has taken possession of that little ditch and placed the countryman's plantation on its bank, quadrupling its value. And that other party's formally valuable plantation finds itself away out yonder on a big island. The old water course around it will soon shoal up. Boats cannot approach within ten miles of it, and down goes its value to a fourth of its former worth. Watches are kept on those narrow necks at needful times, and if a man happens to be caught cutting a ditch across them the chances are all against his ever having another opportunity to cut a ditch."

As levees would become more common to contain the river during times of flood, a man fearing his land would be flooded would occasionally cross the river with dynamite to blow up a levee on the other side to flood that land and ease the pressure on his own levee.

Armed men patrolling the levees in times of flood became a tradition. As late as 1994 a man was convicted of blowing up a levee during a great flood in the Mississippi Valley, flooding thousands of acres and farm houses because, as he testified at his trial, he wanted to strand his wife on the other side.

29. THE GREAT FLOOD OF 1882

There have been many devastating floods on the great rivers. The flood of 1882 was particularly awful. As the waters continued to rise; a newspaper in New Orleans, *The Times Democrat*, sent a relief steamer and a reporter to the far reaches. Here now is a portion of a story the paper printed on March 29, 1882. It is joyless:

"One does not appreciate the sight of earth until he has traveled through a flood. At sea, one does not expect to look for it, but here with fluttering leaves, shadowy forest aisles, housetops barely visible, it is expected. In fact, a graveyard if mounds were above water would be appreciated. The river here is known only because there is an opening in the trees, and then at all.

"At thirty miles above the mouth of Black River the water extends from Natchez on the Mississippi across to the pine hills of Louisiana, a distance of 73 miles. And there is hardly a spot that is not ten feet under water.

"As we progress, habitations become more frequent, but are yet still miles apart. Nearly all of them are deserted and the outhouses floated off. To add to the gloom, almost every living thing seems to have departed. And not a whistle of a bird, nor the bark of a squirrel, can be heard in the solitude.

"Down the river floats now a neatly whitewashed henhouse, then a cluster of neatly split fence rails, or a door, and a bloated carcass solemnly guarded by a pair of buzzards, the only bird to be seen, which feasts on the carcass as it bears them along. A picture frame, in which there was a cheap lithograph of a soldier on horseback, as it floated on told of some hearth invaded by the water and despoiled of this ornament.

"In order to save coal, as it was impossible to get that fuel at any point that we touched during the expedition, a lookout was kept for a wood pile. Presently a little girl, not certainly over twelve years, paddled out in the smallest little canoe and handled it with all the deftness of an old voyager. The little one looked more like an Indian girl than a white child, and laughed when asked if she were afraid. She had been raised in the pirogue and could go anywhere. She was bound out to pick willow leaves for the stock, and she pointed to a house nearby with water three inches deep on the floors. At its back door was moored a raft about thirty feet square with a sort of fence built upon it and, inside of this, some sixteen cows and twenty hogs were standing. The family did not complain, except on account of losing their stock, and promptly brought us a supply of wood on a flat.

"An old man in a pirogue was asked how the willow leaves agreed with his cattle. He stopped in his work, and with an ominous shake of his head replied 'well sure, it's enough to keep warmth in your bodies, and that's all we expect. But it's hard on the hogs, particularly the small ones. They're droppin' off powerful fast. But what can you do? It's all we got.'

"Taking a skiff with the general, your reporter was pulled up to a little house of two rooms in which the water was standing two feet on the floors. In one of the large rooms were huddled the horses and cows of the place. While in the other, the widow Taylor and her son were seated on a scaffold raised on the floor. One or two dugouts were drifting about in the room ready to be put in service at any time. When the flat was brought up, the side of the house was cut away as the only means of getting the animals out, and the cattle were driven onboard the boat. General York,* in this as in every case, inquired if the family desired to leave. Informing them that Major Burke, of the Times Democrat, had sent *The Susie* up for that purpose. Mrs. Taylor said she thanked Major Burke, but she would try and hold out.

"The remarkable tenacity of the people here to their homes, it is beyond all comprehension. After weeks of privation and suffering, people still cling to their houses and leave only when there is not room between the water and the ceiling to build a scaffold on which to stand. It seems to be incomprehensible, yet the love for the old place was stronger than that for safety.

"All along Black River, *The Susie* has been visited by scores of planters whose tales are the repetition of those already heard of suffering and loss. An old-timer, who has lived on the river since 1844, said there never was such a rise. The flood here is rising about three and a half inches every twenty-four hours, and rains have set in which will increase this. All are working night and day, and *The Susie* hardly has time to stop for more than an hour anywhere.

*former Confederate general, Zebulon York

"Reports have come in that a woman and child have been washed away below here, and two cabins floated off. Their occupants are the same who refused to come off day before yesterday. One would not believe the utter passiveness of the people."

Over a century later, and as hard as we've tried, there is still little control of flooding in the vast river valleys, but nothing approaching the thousands of square miles of devastation as here described.

30. NEW ORLEANS

And we notice such distinction between the poor planters, who lived along the rivers' banks, and bustling commerce in the major cities, such as New Orleans. Mark Twain described:

"It was always the custom for the boats to leave New Orleans between four and five o'clock in the afternoon. From three o'clock onward they'd be burning rosin and pitch pine as a sign of preparation. And so one had the picturesque spectacle of a rank, some two or three miles long, of tall ascending columns of coal black smoke.

"A colonnade, which supported a sable roof of the same smoke, blended together and spreading abroad over the city. Every outward boat had its flag flying at the jack staff, and sometimes a duplicate on the bird staff astern. Two or three miles of Mates are commanding and swearing with more than usual emphasis, countless processions of freight barrels and boxes are spinning atop the levee, and flying aboard the stage plank the latest passengers were dodging and skipping among these frantic things hoping to reach the forecastle companionway alive, but having their doubts about it.

"Women with reticules and bam boxes were trying to keep up with husbands freighted with carpet sacks and crying babies, and making a failure of it by losing their heads in the whirl and roar and general distraction.

"Drays and baggage vans were clattering hither and thither in a wild hurry, every now and then getting blocked and jammed together. Then for ten seconds one could not see them for the profanity, except vaguely and dimly. Every windless connected to every forehatch, from one end of that long array of steamboats to the other, was keeping up a deafening wiz and whirl, lowering freight into the hold, and the half-naked crews of perspiring Negros that worked them were roaring such songs as *Da Lass Sack, Da Lass Sack, Da Lass Sack*, inspired to unimaginable exhalations by the chaos of turmoil and racket that was driving everybody else mad.

"By this time the hurricane boiler decks of the steamers would be packed and black with passengers. The last bells would beginning to clang all down the line, and then the pow-wow seemed to double. In a moment or two the final warning came, a simultaneous din of Chinese gongs with the cry: *All That Ain't Goin'-- Please to go Ashore*, and behold the pow-wow quadrupled. People came swarming ashore, overturning excited stragglers that were trying to swarm aboard one more moment. After a long array of stage planks were being hauled in, each with its customary latest passenger clinging to the end of it with teeth, nails and everything else, and the customary latest procrastinator making a wild spring shoreward over his head.

"Now a number of boats would backwards into the stream, leaving wide gaps in the scurried ranks of steamers. Citizens crowd the decks of boats that are not to go in order to see the sights. Steamer after steamer straightens herself up, gather all her strength, and presently comes swinging by under a tremendous head of steam. The flag flying, black smoke rolling, and her entire crew of firemen and deckhands massed together on the forecastle, the best voice in the lot hollering from the mist, being mounted on the capstan, waving his hat or a flag and all roaring a mighty chorus while the parting cannons boom and the multitudinous spectators swing their hats and huzzas. Steamer after steamer falls into line and the stately procession goes winging its flight up the river."

31. THE MEAN CAPTAIN

Mark Twain loved to tell a humorous story, and he loved it even better when the story was a true one about the river. A Twain favorite was a story about a pilot he once only identified as Steven. But before we hear it, remember two things: when underway, the pilot is always in command, even over the captain. And, when going up stream, boats never take the center of the river because the current there is much stronger.

"Once a pretty mean captain caught Steven in New Orleans out of work and, as usual, out of money. He had laid steady siege to Steven, who was in a very close place, and finally persuaded him to hire with him at one-hundred and twenty-five dollars a month, just half wages. The captain agreeing not to divulge the secret and so bring down the contempt of all the guild upon the poor fellow. But the boat was not more than a day out of New Orleans before Steven discovered that the captain was boasting of his exploit and that all the officers had been told. Steven winced, but said nothing.

"About the middle of the afternoon the captain stepped out on the hurricane deck, cast his eye around and looked a good deal surprised. He glanced inquiringly aloft at Steven, but Steven was whistling placidly and attending to his business.

"The captain stood around awhile in evident discomfort and once or twice seemed about to make a suggestion. But the etiquette of the river taught him to avoid that sort of rashness and so he managed to hold his peace. He chaffed and puzzled a few minutes longer, then retired to his apartments. But soon he was out again and apparently more perplexed than ever. Presently he ventured to remark with deference, 'pretty good stage of the river now, aint't it sir?'

"And Steven relied, 'Well, I should say so. Banks full is a pretty liberal stage.'

"And the captain said, 'seems to be a good deal of current here.'

"And Steven replied, 'good deal don't describe it, it's worse than a millrace.'

"And the captain said, 'isn't it easier in toward shore than it is out here in the middle?'

"And Steven replied, 'yes, I reckon it is, but a body can't be too careful with a steamboat. It's pretty safe out here. Can't strike any bottom here, you can depend on that.'

"Well, the captain departed, looking rueful enough. At this rate he'd probably die of old age before his boat got to St. Louis.

"Next day he appeared on deck and again and found Steven faithfully standing up the middle of the river, fighting the whole vast force of the Mississippi, and whistling the same placid tune.

"This thing was becoming serious. In by the shore was a slower boat clipping along in the easy water and gaining steadily. She began to make for an island chute. Steven stuck to the middle of the river.

"Speech was wrung from the captain, he said "mister, don't that chute cut off a good deal of distance?'

"And Steven replied, 'Well, I think it does, but I don't know.'

"And the captain said 'don't know? Well, isn't there water enough in it now to go through?'

"And Steven replied, 'I expect there is, but I'm not certain.'

"And the captain said, 'upon my word, this is odd, those pilots in that boat yonder are going to try it. You mean to say that you don't know as much as they do?'

"And Steven replied, 'They [laughing], they? Why, they are two-hundred and fifty dollar pilots. But don't you be uneasy, I know as much as any man can afford to know for a hundred and twenty-five.'

"The captain surrendered. Five minutes later Steven was boiling through the chute and showing the rival boat a two-hundred and fifty dollar pair of heels."

32. WHEN RIVER FREIGHT WAS KING

Passenger traffic on the rivers was exciting, but freight spurred the economic growth of the expanding United States. As an example of how efficient at moving coal were these barges, hear this news item printed in the *Cincinnati Commercial* in 1882:

"The towboat *Joseph B. Williams* is on her way to New Orleans with a tow of thirty-two barges containing six-hundred thousand bushels, seventy-six pounds to the bushel, of coal exclusive of her own fuel, being the largest tow ever taken to New Orleans, or anywhere else in the world.

"Her freight bill, at three cents a bushel, amounts to eighteen-thousand dollars. It would take eighteen-hundred [railroad] cars, of three-hundred and thirty-three bushels to the car, to transport this amount of coal. At ten dollars per ton, or a hundred a car, which would be a fair price for distance by rail, the freight bill would amount to a hundred and eighty thousand dollars, or a hundred and sixty-two thousand more by rail than by river.

"The tow will be taken from Pittsburg to New Orleans in fourteen or fifteen days. It would take one-hundred trains of eighteen cars to the train to transport this one tow of six-hundred thousand bushel of coal. And even if it made the usual speed of fast freight lines, it would take one whole summer to put it through by rail."

33. GRADUAL DEMISE

A lot of people blamed the railroads for the gradual demise of steamboat commerce, but that wasn't the only problem. The words of Mark twain:

"If you send a damned fool to St. Louis, and you don't tell them he's a damned fool, they'll never find it out. There's one thing sure, if I had a damned fool I should know what to do with him. Ship him to St. Louis. It's the noblest market in the word for that kind of property."

When Twain wrote those words he was faulting St. Louis, and the other major river cities, for crippling steamboat trade.

"River towns will manage to find and use a chance here and there to cripple and retard their progress. They kept themselves back in the days of steamboat supremacy by a system of wharfage dues, so stupidly graded as to prohibit what may be called small retail traffic in freights and passengers. Boats were charged such heavy wharfage that they could not afford to land for one or two passengers or a light lot of freight.

"Instead of encouraging the bringing of trade to their doors, the towns diligently and effectively discouraged it. They could have had many boats and low rates, but their policy rendered few boats and high rates compulsory. It is a policy which extends from New Orleans to St. Paul."

And this made things tough for the owners, who also were often the captain and pilot, as told by Captain Heckmann: "… locally here on the Gasconade River, the captain received the enormous sum of seventy-five dollars a month,. And he acted as pilot, master, and deckhand … he helped carry wheat. And he got his board when the boat was out of port, when he came in home he boarded himself.

"I worked long enough to acquire a little money and bought a half interest in an old tugboat. And we had the boat chartered [to] different contractors. Sometimes we'd have it chartered to the Army Engineers. And we were making good wages, good money. I wasn't satisfied. So I went into the big boat business. I decided to build a big boat [at the time, largest on the Missouri River] to operate as a freight boat from St. Louis to beyond Jefferson City, up by Rocheport, took a week running daylight."

Captain Heckmann had christened the steamer the *John Heckmann*. In 1995 his daughter, Dorothy Heckmann Shrader [born Dec. 3, 1913] wrote me she remembered as a child in the 1920s: "My father had the worst case of real steamboat fever of any of the Heckmann boys. Just how he conceived and built the largest boat on the Missouri River (built by private funds) and eyeballed the whole project,* made it work –this is a mystery to me and I was right there when it happened."

34. EXCURSIONS, PROHIBITION, AND LIQUOR

Captain Heckmann told me that as freight became unprofitable the only thing left would be the excursion business for the *John Heckmann*, as we have today. But he said excursion boats often fell

---

*Captain Heckmann's grandson, John Shrader, wrote me in 1995 that in building the steamer, "as was common then, Grandfather didn't use plans…"

on hard times too: "We operated [it as a] a freight boat on the Illinois, [and] on the Cumberland River out of Nashville, way up into the mountains. Then after we found out we couldn't make any money as a freight boat, then we converted her. Took the cabin out and put a dance floor on the second deck, and bought a deck and made an excursion boat.

"Sounds like big business, ya know, you get seventy-five cents apiece for about a three hour trip, mostly at night, sometimes run twice a day. But the only trouble we had on the excursion boat was booze. It was during Prohibition days, ya know … keep booze off because you can get [in trouble with the law]. Then if you have a guy selling booze you're going to have a couple fights on your hands. So that was our big trouble. We had to check 'em as they come aboard, ya know, and if they have booze on 'em just take it away from them, there wasn't a thing they could do, just throw it overboard.

"It looked like nice easy money, but it never dawned on me that you had your advertising to pay for, you had a crew of about fourteen men had to be paid for, you had to buy and burn so much fuel every day, and you had to hire an orchestra. You paid the orchestra whether you made a trip or not. If it rained and you got rained out, the orchestra got paid just the same. So some days we'd make a little money and some days we wouldn't make a darn thing. And that's where my mistakes started. From then on I just … I had made a lot of mistakes before but I never really made any big mistakes until I came back here. I never could make any more than payroll and just about balance even."

His daughter, Dorothy, remembered: "We all slaved for nine years to keep that steamer afloat. It was just too much boat, too late, but dad was the eternal optimist—he never gave up. We sure did not do it for the money—there wasn't any."

And when the steamer's end came it was heartbreaking for the whole family, as Captain Heckmann told me: "And I kept that up until the boat was finally ... had her laid up for the winter down here east of town along a rock shore. Ice practically closed the channel off that winter and that was one of the darnedest ice jams you ever saw. That gorge let go and the river fell about eight feet. And I'm telling you, after it was over, it just looked like some giant had come along and he just put his foot on every deck and flattened her out."

35. LICENSE TO PILOT MORE RIVER THAN ANYONE

The late Captain Ed Heckmann was the last of the great riverboat pilots, with a license to pilot more river than anyone who has ever lived, including his famous brother Steamboat Bill. Just prior to his death he told us how it came about: "It's quite a long story how I acquired those licenses. A pilot is licensed for a certain section of the river. Take for instance, Kermit [Baecker] goes up for his first license. They may give him a license from St. Louis to Jefferson City or to Kansas City. He has to show his knowledge of that section of the river. He has to prove that to 'em. He has to have two men to vouch for him that know something about his ability. Then if he wants to go beyond Kansas City he has to apply for another section, say from Kansas City to Omaha. And that way he gets his extension as he gets the experience, but he has to have the actual experience of being over the river.

"I have experience of having acquired a pilot's license from Fort Benton headwaters to New Orleans. There are several reasons for that. I took a snag boat up the Missouri River before I ever applied to Fort Benton all the way. So I was talking to the inspector, Captain Alva Day, asked him if he couldn't extend my license to Fort Benton. I said 'you never going to get any boats up there if you don't have men to run 'em, and if you know a hundred miles of Missouri river you know it all. Because you never *know* it, you just have to learn it.' So I applied for a license to Fort Benton and he gave me the license.

"Then finally I had license to Cairo [Illinois] and about a hundred miles of the Illinois River. My Illinois license extended to Joliet, which is not far from Chicago. And my Mississippi license, I had a license for about a hundred miles above St. Louis. I had that extended all the way to New Orleans. Then the harbor of New Orleans, I had to take a special examination. They give ya examination for in the harbor of New Orleans, you know. You have to know a compass course, run in the fog which I never tried to do. So that's the way I acquired the license all the way from the head waters of the Missouri to New Orleans. The reason the old time pilots didn't have that type of license is because they confined their work to the Missouri River. By the time they made a trip up the Missouri River the season was about over and they didn't have time to ply the river to New Orleans, they had no occasion to.

"In the meantime I acquired a Master's License. You have to serve a year as pilot or a year as First Mate before you can apply for a Master's. The Master's was for all tonnage, for all rivers. And about the second year I was in Alaska and I had my pilot's license extended to cover the Yukon River and all the tributaries, about six-thousand miles of water, so that makes my licenses [totally] unique."

Hermann, it was said, was the busiest port on the Missouri River during Captain Heckmann's active years. His grandson, John Shrader, wrote me in 1995: " ... shortly before he died, I asked him if he would like piloting today on the Missouri. He said 'no, there's nothing going on now.' I replied 'but Grand Dad, I see boats running barges up and down the river all the time.' His response was 'Oh John, the romance is all gone now. Anymore, it's just a business.' This, as much as anything I remember him saying, summarized his abundant charm and his exasperating impracticality."

36. EPILOGUE

Hermann is a sleepy town today. The river traffic passes but now seldom ever stops. Its indefatigable and incomparable steamboat pilot, Captain Edward Heckmann, died at his home there in early 1974 and not long before his 90th birthday. I am among the legions of people most honored to have known him. To this day, in that city on a bluff overlooking the Missouri River, stands a replica of a pilothouse with the wheel of his last steamboat, the *John Heckmann*, as a loving tribute to his memory.

For deeper insights, the student may wish to read works authored by Steamboat Bill Heckmann, *Sixty-five Years of Steamboating on the Missouri River*, and other material gathered by the late Dorothy Heckmann Shrader [1913—2004] in her books, *Steamboat Legacy, Steamboat Fever, Steamboat Kid*, and her other writings.

Captain Heckmann's voice and stories are edited from an interview he granted at his home in Hermann, Missouri, in late 1973. Also recorded that day was material from his friend and fellow pilot, the late Captain Kermit Baecker. Other reenactments are written for this book with facts gleaned from various historical accounts and archives of those days.

This production is duplicated in audio on *iTunes* and *Amazon Audible* [**FREE** with Audible trial at Amazon. www.RiverboatYears.com/col] in living stereo with Captain Heckmann's actual voice, appropriate sound effects, and where the characters seem to come alive. It is historically accurate in content, effects, and mood.

Colonel Mason

ACKNOWLEDGEMENTS

Deepest thanks to the late Captain Kermit Baecker [1909—1996] who introduced me to Captain Edward Heckmann just brief months before Heckmann's death. My sincere gratitude also goes to Captain Heckmann's late daughter, Dorothy, and her son, John Shrader, who contributed unique memories. Plus none of the audio work would have been done so well without Lynn Crochet, the talented digital recording engineer who first produced this book in audio and created most all its sound effects.

Credits on Audio Production
[in living stereo, now available on iTunes and Amazon Audible]

Voice and words of Captain Edward Heckmann
    His Own
Voice and words of Captain Kermit Baecker
    His Own
All Other Voices, including Twain's
    Colonel Mason
Words from *Life on the Mississippi*
    Mark Twain
Historical research and verification
    Colonel Mason
Script and Editing
    Colonel Mason
Audio Production
    Lynn Crochet
Sound Effects
    Lynn Crochet
Audio re-mastering in 2019 from original recording
    Colonel Mason
Graphic Designs
    Jill Snead
Cover Art
    Abdellah Askane

INDEX, noted by chapter

Alaska: 64
Alton, Illinois: 3
Amazon Audible: 36
Amazon River: 1, 25
Americans, native: 3
Arkansas, state: 28
Ashishishe, Crow scout: 25
Atlantic, ocean: 3

Baecker, Kermit—captain: 1, 12, 35
Barges: 3, 14, 32, 35
Baton Rouge: 2
Bavaria: 1
Bellefontaine Cemetery: 23
Benteen, Army Capt.: 25
Bighorn, river: 25
Bismarck, ND: 25
Black, George: 21
Black River, the: 29
Boatmen, early: 3, 5
Boilers: 21, 25, 27, 30
Boston, Mass: 3
Broadhorns: 3
Burke, major: 29

Campbell, Dave—pilot: 25
Canada: 3
Cave-in-Rock, cutthroats: 7
China: 3
Chutes: 13, 31
Cincinnati Commercial, newspaper: 32
Civil War: 17
Clemens, Henry: 21
Clemens, Samuel Langhorn: 23
Council of Trent: 3
Cromwell, Oliver: 3
Cumberland River: 34
Curly, Crow scout: 25

Custer, massacre: 25
Cutoffs: 28

Day, Alva—captain: 35
De Soto: 3

Dianna, steamboat: 26

Ealer, George--pilot: 21
Engineers, Army: 33
Engineers, steamers: 21, 24, 25
Europeans: 3

Far West, steamboat: 25
Faulk, George—engineer: 25
Firemen: 25, 32
First Mate: 19, 35
Floods: 28. 29
Fort Benton, MT: 35
Fort Buford, ND: 25
Fort Stevenson, ND: 25
Freight: 9, 14, 24, 30, 32, 33, 34
French explorers: 3

Gamblers: 5, 6, 8
Gasconade River: 33
Gibbon, Army general: 25
Gold Rush: 15
Grant, Army general: 18
Great Lakes: 3
Green Bay, Wisconsin: 3
Gulf of California: 3
Gulf of Mexico: 3

Hannibal, Missouri: 1, 10
Harlots: 7
Harper's: 18

68

Heckmann, Edward—captain: 1, 8, 9, 12, 15, 16, 17, 20, 21, 25, 33, 34, 35, 36
Heckmann, William—captain: 1, 3, 8, 16, 21, 35, 36
Hermann, Missouri: 1, 7, 16, 35
Hurricane Deck: 17, 30, 31

Immaculate Conception, Feast of: 3
Indians: 3, 6, 15, 20, 29
Inquisition, Spanish: 3
Island number 37: 7
Island number 74: 28
Island number 92: 28

James, Jesse: 7
Jefferson City, MO: 33
John Heckmann, steamboat: 33, 34, 35, 36
Joliet, Illinois: 35
Jolliet, Louis: 3
Joseph B. Williams, towboat: 32

Kansas City, MO: 35
Keelboats: 3
Keokuk, IW: 10
Klinefelter, captain: 21
Klondike : 15

La Salle; 3
Leadman: 12
Levee House: 1
Little Bighorn, river: 25
Louisiana: 18, 28, 29

Mark Twain: 1, 3, 5, 6, 7, 10, 11, 12, 13, 14, 17, 18, 19, 20, 21, 22, 23, 24, 26, 27, 28, 31.
Marsh, Grant—Capt: 25
Marquette, priest: 3
Mary Queen of Scots: 3
Master's License: 35
Memphis, TN: 4, 21
Michelangelo: 3

Mississippi, Basin, 2, 28
Mississippi, River: 1, 3, 4, 9, 10, 14, 15, 16, 18, 21, 22, 24, 26, 28, 29, 31, 35
Mississippi, state: 7, 18, 28
Missouri, River: 1, 3, 15, 16, 21, 25, 27, 33, 35
Missouri, State: 3, 7, 10, 23, 28, 35
Murrell, John—outlaw, 7

Natchez, Mississippi: 7, 9, 29
Natchez, steamboat: 1, 24, 25
Native Americans: 3, 6, 15, 20, 29
New Madrid Fault, the: 4
New Orleans, Louisiana: 1, 3, 5, 7, 9, 11, 16, 24, 30, 31, 32, 33, 35
New Orleans, **Picayune**, 23
New Orleans, **True Delta**, 23
Ohio, river: 7, 21, 26
Ohio, state: 25
Omaha, NB: 35
Outlaws: 7
Ozarks: 1

Pacific coast: 23
Packet boats: 9, 10
Pennsylvania, steamboat: 21
Pilots: 1, 3, 5, 8, 10, 11, 12, 13, 14, 15, 16, 17, 19, 20, 21, 23, 24, 25, 26, 31, 33, 35
Pirogue: 29
Pittsburg, coal flat: 5, 32
Pittsburg, PA: 14
Posey County, Indiana: 14
Prohibition: 34

Quixote, Don: 3

Racing: 24
Railroad, the: 6, 32, 33
Reading the water: 1, 20
Reefs: 8, 20, 26
Reelfoot Lake: 4
Reno, Army Major: 25

Rhineland, 1
Robert E. Lee, steamboat: 1, 24, 25
Rocheport, MO: 33
Ruffians: 7

St. Louis, Missouri: 1, 4, 7, 9, 10, 15, 16, 23, 24, 25, 26, 27, 31, 33, 35
St. Paul, MN: 33
Scows: 14
Sellers, Isaiah–captain: 23
Shakespeare: 3
Ship Island: 21
Shrader, Dorothy Heckmann: 1, 33, 35
Shrader, John: 35
Side-wheelers: 8, 21
Silver Street: 7
Sistine Chapel: 3
Slaves: 7, 18
Snags: 14, 15, 21, 25
Spanish, explorers: 3,
Spanish, Inquisition: 3
Steamboat Bill: 1, 3, 8, 16, 21, 35, 36
Sternwheelers: 8
Stone Hill Winery: 1

Telegraph: 23, 25
Terry, Army general: 25
Thieves: 7
Thompson, Ben—First Mate: 25
Times Democrat, The: 29
Trappers: 4
Trent, Council of: 3

Union forces: 18
United States, of America: 3
Upper River: 26, 28

Vicksburg, Mississippi: 18
Virginia, Sea of: 3

Whiskey: 6

Yazoo River: 18
Yellowstone, river: 25
Youngstown, Ohio: 25
Yukon: 15, 35

Historic Hermann Museum

312 Schiller at Fourth Street • 573-486-2017
For Group Tours Call 573-486-0110

Visit the Museum & Gift Shop

Open Third Weekend of March through October
PLUS November Weekends & First Two Weekends of December

Hours: 10:00 to 4:00 Daily
Noon to 4:00 Sunday • Closed Wednesday

Blue Star Museum — Free admission for active military and immediate family

www.HistoricHermann.com